T0195585

YOU
ARE THE NEXT
BILLIONAIRE

YOU

ARE THE NEXT

BILLIONAIRE

Stand Up, Think More, Think Bigger Than Yourself,
and Have the Will to Self-Lift in Business

**MIGUEL TZOC, TETZAGUIC
AMADEO VASQUEZ
JOHN MSEKE, HAKIZIMANA**

YOU ARE THE NEXT BILLIONAIRE
STAND UP, THINK MORE, THINK BIGGER THAN YOURSELF,
AND HAVE THE WILL TO SELF-LIFT IN BUSINESS

iUniverse books may be ordered through booksellers or by contacting:

iUniverse
1663 Liberty Drive
Bloomington, IN 47403
www.iuniverse.com
1-800-Authors (1-800-288-4677)

Because of the dynamic nature of the Internet, any web addresses or links contained in this book may have changed since publication and may no longer be valid. The views expressed in this work are solely those of the author and do not necessarily reflect the views of the publisher, and the publisher hereby disclaims any responsibility for them.

Any people depicted in stock imagery provided by Thinkstock are models, and such images are being used for illustrative purposes only. Certain stock imagery © Thinkstock.

ISBN: 978-1-5320-4176-1 (sc)
ISBN: 978-1-5320-4177-8 (e)

Library of Congress Control Number: 2018901136

Print information available on the last page.

iUniverse rev. date: 01/24/2018

Contents

INVESTMENT

Step One: Business Investment

One must learn about the major challenges to starting a business and successively managing before actually starting the business. My friend and I had an idea to open a business. We thought about opening a business for a long time. One day passed, then two days, then months. Years passed, and we still had the same idea to open a business. Finally, after hard work, calculations, investment, and planning, we took four steps. Step one was a business investment plan. Step two was a business plan. Step three was finding the food truck and negotiations. Step four was putting the plan in action.

Investment is always having a plan, always having to be at the top. Economic growth can be inspiring through its use on a business level. When the company contracts or acquires a new piece of production equipment in order to raise the total output of a good facility, the increased production can cause the gross natural. This allows the economy to grow and generate a lot of money through increased production, based on previous equipment investment. The more you invest, the more you should plan what comes next. Money will come later. Don't worry about money; it always comes. If you work for more money investments and always see the big picture, then when follow up with action and regularly schedule divergent, big-picture thinking, you can bring new, better results, giving you confidence that the small things you are doing every day work along the right path.

Without investment, there is no business to open. People who want to open a business must have money to start that business. Our food truck business needed more money than we had anticipated. You can have a vision, yet a vison without mathematics it is a useless vision. You should carefully think about it first. We set a goal for a financial plan. Both of us checked our accounts and what we gained each month. From there on, we had a picture of how much each of us could invest in this food truck business. It took month after month, yet we still focused on the goal and the achievement of the idea. Never quit in your vision to succeed. At that time, Tzoc was already financially secure. He had painting deals, and he had livestock in Guatemala. Oh, did I forget to tell you that he had a job and went to school at the same time?

Starting a business does not mean education in business has to be achieved. Even though having that little bit of education in business is helpful, most of the time you can do the basic functions. Those functions can be learned by self-teaching. You can teach yourself by reading books, attending seminars of business of your interest, or talking to people who are doing what you hope to do. If Tzoc was an ordinary person, he would not have those businesses, yet he'd still be able to attend school and have a side job. After having a business, ordinary people stop working, even for themselves. They hire someone to do the work they are supposed to be doing. That is one of the advantage of having a business. You have other people doing your dirty and even clean duties. I know you don't want to be an ordinary person. Corner your neighbor business. Deposit your business neighbor's profits straight in to your business bank account. With that hard commitment to stand tall in business, Tzoc he is still working hard on other sides of business. Tzoc invested seven thousand dollars, Amadeo invested five thousand. And I, Zeit, invested two thousand. After the first investment for start-up, we still had to continue paying for the food truck. It was under a down payment system. If you think starting a business is easy, then you have to redefine what you think of business. It is not easy, but it is achievable.

We started with fourteen thousand dollars. We still had to pay for it via a down payment. Know when you are taking a mortgage, a loan, or a down payment, always think about it. The seller will use all forms of manipulation to make sure the item is sold. If the item is sold, then he deposits your down payment into his account. If you didn't give yourself time to think about it, then you fall into risky traps, which you could avoid. Before signing the papers of a contract or mortgage, think twice. If you think once, then you will be thinking the second time when the deposit you made is in their bank account. It will be like you are transferring money from your saving account to your checking account, except you will be wiring the money to *their* account. That will terrify you if you don't think twice.

Why the Business Investment Plan First?

You might be wondering why you should do the investment plan first. You need to invest and create a plan where you save money for your idea. You might have an idea that is really great and will put you at the top, but if you don't have any money invested in that idea, the ideas is useless. You might have investors who invest in the new idea, but if you don't have investors and didn't save any money, the idea is worthless. How can you make sure that your idea is not worthless?

When you have the idea, it should be profitable, beneficial, and cash generating. If your idea is not profitable, why would you even start that business? The idea is worthless, and you will be spending more money and losing support because your idea cannot generate profit. In business, we all know the fundamental law is to make a profit. Your idea must be useful, and it must be rewarding after the hard work that you have put into it. It must yield some profit, it must put you on the next level. It must not let you down. I know you will have ups and downs while starting up your business idea, putting it in action, and trying to schedule yourself to the next level, but don't give up. Make sure that it's beneficial and rewarding after the hard work. When you have worked hard, after a couple of months or years, your idea should put you in a place where you can have back the time that you put in when you started the business. It should give you financial freedom and time for you to spend on other things. Maybe you can go to the next idea, open the next business, or expand your business that you already have.

Your idea must be profitable. If it is not profitable, then there is no need to put it in action or start it at all. It must give you advantages, such as opening that idea in different locations. For example, Starbucks is everywhere, and at each corner you will see a Starbucks. They had a great idea to sell coffee to young adults, adults, and even children. Starbucks is large and is expanding its wings across the world. Starbucks has over 23,770 locations worldwide, from China to Canada, the United Kingdom, the United States, and Japan. The company started on the West Coast of the United States in Seattle, Washington. That is 4,869 miles from Japan. Yet they still went to that country, and they've expanded their wings in South Korea. I think if they had a chance to sell their coffee in North Korea, they would because the product or service that you offer is the key. In most civilized countries, coffee is needed. People like to stay awake, and they want to stay focused.

You need a business idea that will propel you to the next level, not an idea that will let you down. When you're in business, you need to have patience. It takes time to generate that profit and get back the money that you invested, but it's worth it. Take measured steps by first starting to invest your idea. Do research and try to figure out what is out there. What is bad about your idea, and what is good about it? Don't feel let down, like we did. The food trailer business idea was a perfect idea at that moment, and we took steps and made some measurements so that we didn't feel dumb quickly. But because we took our steps so fast, we didn't do our research deeply. We fell down, which is okay. It gave us a new, brilliant way. I knew a way to envision the business.

Step Two: A Business Plan

Allocate Time to Think

Everything sounds very differet because every day has a different mind goal. If you allow yourself to do what is your next step in your list, you'll never find the time to see the big picture. Always do something that feels urgent in order to see the big picture in the end. There is always a light to success.

We mapped our goals and what we wanted to achieve with the food truck business.

We started writing up a business summary: market analysis, target market, type of food, start cost, business locations, local competitors, management summary, cash flow, profit and loss, and conclusions. That was our food truck business plan. You need a written plan that helps you track the development of your company. What needs to change? What is selling? What is your position in the market? Business plans need updates across all business objectives.

Before starting, you must have that plan with you. Where will you be going without knowing where you are heading? You will be lost. The business sphere is big. First, map your goals, like a mapping with dots. Keep track of all the left and right turns. If you don't keep up with those dots, then you will be lost. In business, it is the same as taking a journey using GPS. GPS always has turns and corners. The first corner will follow the second corner. In business, the same principle has to be followed.

Amadeo once asked a question that I will never forget. "Why do we have only one goal?" That question is interesting and refreshing. We looked at the paper where we were mapping the goals. The eight steps of operating the business had similarities. Amadeo added, "Look at all this boletes we have here for the operation of the business. They are the same." That is when we saw the repetition of the same action. In business, directing functions makes up the business. Just remember that they have to be a little similar in order for them to intertwine, for better and smoother business management. We checked the dot goal paper and started over.

After mapping our road on the paper, we then set long-term and short-term goals. By separating short-term goals with long-term goals, you can have a great road map on what you should focus on for starting, and what you should do afterward. We had some perfect strategies on how we would process our business and how we would be unique and skillful. You need a strategy. One of our killer ideas was the ability to advertise our food before we could even test it. We used to do publicity one month to two weeks before opening the business. Our strategies were greater than the food truck businesses that already existed. People always ask themselves, "How will customers know that I am open?" Well, you already have the answer. Do the publicity before you show up. Put out the time and date you will be opening your business. That helps you get more customers when you open, and it helps you make connections. Making some or all of the customers your daily customers. Have discounts. The research should never stop. We did some research and asked some questions here and there about food truck business. We asked those questions to food truck business owners and customers who bought food at the food trucks, so that we could get a glimpse into the business to which we were committing ourselves. It is not easy for other business owners to give you a view of how they run their businesses, because most of that information is confidential. We tested different types of recipes from food made in food trucks. We had a test and an idea of what business we were putting ourselves into, which required a long-term commitment.

The only way to succeed in business is that you must commit yourself to the idea that you're putting yourself into it. Our priority was to our customers, and our focus was on our recipes. We planned some great recipes that were not around in the areas. We cooked fajitas, shrimp, chicken, salmon, wings, and burgers, and we served shakes as well. We were different from our competitors. We had customers from different races. Even those who disliked food truck businesses, like President Donald Trump, came to eat our delicious menus. We were the only food truck that cooked those types of recipes in our area.

We all have challenges in our lives and in our businesses. In business, you face many challenges: negotiation, competition, shortage of capital, critical business plan, coming up with a product or service that is in high demand, hiring or firing employees, and management of the business operation. Those are just few situations that can be found in the business sphere. You must fight these challenges. If you refuse to attend to them, then starting the business was just a play. In business, don't let those situations repeal your commitment to achieving that dream. Be the keeper of your post and have a plan before jumping into opening your company.

Action First

If I have a big goal, I will generally procrastinate on tackling it, unless I immediately choose the first step. If you want to create a car, I want make sure you know how they made the first car, and you should make mine totally differently with new tecnology that people can buy from you in order to become succesfull and kick the other company's ass.

Generate Ideas

I often start thinkging on a big process by asking, "What is my most ambitious goal?" The strongest outcome of thinking big is being able to step outside your confort zone, away from the day-to-day routine. Ideas can take a long time to reach the path to success.

No One Can Take Care of Your Business Like You

Nobody can take care of your business like you. You are the best in your motivation. You are the one on the journey to the moon. Great thing will happen for you and because of you. Everybody is afraid of losing money in business; all is risk. Those who want to be in business most have a passion and never lose hope. When life gives you something that makes you feel afraid, that's you have a chance to grow strong and be brave. Bill Belichick is a coach for the New England Patriots, who were in Super Bowl LI against the Atlanta Falcons. At the end of the third quarter, New England was losing badly. It was not very easy to come back for the win.

The Falcons were very happy because they were very close to getting the championship. All Falcons fans were already celebrating the victory. Belichick, New England's head coach, knew that the game was not over yet, and it was not the first Super Bowl they'd played. When the Falcons celebrated because they were winning, Belichick was making a plan to defeat them. No matter how close to success you are, keep fighting and never give up. In the fourth quarter, the game was tight in the last second of regular time. The Falcons were almost the winners of the Super Bowl.

The unbelievable game went to overtime. The Patriots fought and never lost hope when they were losing so badly. In overtime they made a touchdown won the game. Always try, no matter where you want to be. You always want to win, but never lose hope.

Self-motivate, because nobody else will make your plan happen.

It's very simple thing to talk, but you must be in action. It will take time, but keep in mind that nothing is easy in life. Believe what you think and work for it. Anything can happen at any time. You deserve more than others. Keeping that in mind helps your vision to not let anything cross your mind. You will have a concrete mindset. You want have a good lifestyle, which 2 percent of people have. You can do it. Work for it until success is your hands.

It's never too late.

Harland Sanders, the owner of KFC, was born in 1890 and grew up in Indiana. His father died when Harlan was seven years old. His mom remarried when he was twelve. Sanders soon realized he would rather work all day than go to school, and so he dropped out in the seventh grade. Because of his stepfather, things changed for him. Sanders spent the first half of his life in a series of odd jobs. The KFC founder didn't make his remarkable rise to success until his sixties. It's never too late. Everthing can be easier than you think.

There's no perfect time.

If you are waiting for the perfect moment, don't. If you work in construction and see that you will finish but it will take more time to get it done, and you want to leave it for tomorrow, you'd better plan for tomorrow. If you know you can finish today, you'd better get it done because tomorrow will probably rain, and you won't work.

Everyone Starts Somewhere

Nobody is born succesful. Everybody starts somewhere, and there are special people at "the bottom." For example, a chef is faster, but he starts looking and takes action. They never came into a restaurant and started cooking faster. All the businesspeople whom we see at the top started where are you now. They used the foundation steps. One step at the time is key. If you think about a baby who was just born, the baby will not stand and say to its mom, "I am hungry."

It can only get better.

If it is hard at first, it can can only get easier if you have passion in what you believe. Do you like basketball? You go to the gym sometimes to to practice. It will take more time for you to learn, but you set a schedule on what to do. You are going to the gym one hour every day.

Faillture is temporary.

If you fail, you fail. Nobody is born perfect in this world. Most successful people became that way because they kept trying.

Mistakes are learning opportunities.

If you mess up, it's okay. You are learning about what you are working for.

Today is all I can control.

Forget about yesterday. I lost ten thousand dollars. Think about today. Maybe there is a reason you lost the money. Maybe today you can hit the lotto and win a million dollars. Today matters, and yesterday will never come back.

If it were easy, everyone would do it.

Nothing is easy. Easy is for those people who don't want to work for it. Successful people have few friends, read research, and put plans into action. Donald J. Trump sleeps five hours per day because he wants to always be on the top.

Someday is today.

Many people use "someday" to describe the goals. Work hard in silence for today, and not the someday. Those people are not succesful yet, but they are celebrated.

Negative thoughts can't stop me.

If you have a dream about investing, and you are given more time to be successful, then although being tired is normal, you should keep fighting for what you believe. Do what you need to archieve your goals.

Action is a better regret than inaction.

If you have a dream, and you have a passion for it, put it in action. It is very important for you to do something you love to do.

Nobody will take you away from you.

Many successful people achieved their dreams, as can you. If you don't put in action what your dreams are, then everything will come in your mind, and you will regret why you didn't act, but it'll be too late.

You don't need anyone's permission.

In this world, you're born alone, and nobody tells you what to do. You are the one who is responsible for your actons. If you want to be the king of the world, go ahead. If you want to leave some of your signatures on any paper that can destroy the world, you can do it. If you want people to remember you one day, you can do it. It's all on you. Whatever you plan to do, don't wait. Do it!

Finace to Save Money

Saving money is simple. In this country, you work and pay your bills. There are needs and wants.

Both need and want are very important. Need is having the money and investing. Want is not thinking about the next step; you are enjoying life while you can with your money.

Need

To save money, you have to focus more on need. It is very important for you to have a place to sleep and focus on where you want to be in your goals. Transportation is very important. Having you own car is okay. If you don't have a car, you can use buses or bikes to go to work. Many things are difficult to learn, but whenever you're ready to learn, everthing come easy. Saving is simple if you focus on needs first. You will save more more than you think.

Want

Want is just for fun. Want is something that you already have, and you still want it. For example, people go out eat in restaurants because they don't want to cook at home. Wants also include those who go to the movies often.

What Is the Specific Goal?

Think about the big picture. Turn it into a handful of specific goals. This will make it more actionble to work on, and it improves your chance of success. Ambition is taking all the advantages you can to get where you want to be in your next step.

Together as One

Teammates make it better. Both thnk differently, but they always look at a goal together, as one. The best ideas come often because we are always talking about business, and the conversation is interesting. If your teammate brings tremendus ideas, and you do not agree, find a way to bounce the idea straight in order to archieve. If you're in a position to do so, consider asking a buddy. Teammates who don't often get a chance to strategize will be energized by the opportuny to do so with you. Through this exercse, your teammate will get a sense of owership over the conclusion you reach together. Teammates gain focus on what you are doing.

NEGOTIATION

Negotiation is the biggest gun that a man possesses in business. Negotiation is an art that points your vision toward success. I have such incredible experiences, as well as bad ones. Two mind points guarantee an incredible and potential form of your vision.

I'm from Guatemala. I came to the United States with hopes of becoming a member of Wall Street. I had strong ambitions in business, politics, and space exploration. In April 2016, my friends Amadeo Vasquez and Zeit Mseke enrolled in a great deal based on a food truck.

Negotiation deals apply to your daily life. Whether it's buying a house, disputing your cell phone bill, scoring more frequent flier miles, hanging with your girlfriend, paying off your credit card, or negotiating your salary, the basic principles of negotiation are the same. Simply remember that even the most skilled and experienced negotiators will feel discomfort when negotiating. The only difference is that a skilled negotiator has learned to recognize and suppress the outward signs of these feelings. We were enthusiastic, eager, and excited. But remember that you must trust your odds. Sometimes you will face the worst situation, and you want to give up. In April 2016, we had the worst deal ever. We thought that it was a great deal, but we did not trust the odds, and we failed. Believe me, failing at the age of twenty-one wasn't a good experience. We blended a massive amount of money and did not have a way to solve. When you face a problem, there will always be a solution, but you should have faith to solve it.

The best way to negotiate is by never losing your momentum. We keep fighting until we believe that no matter the situation you're in, you still can succeed. Never give up, and trust your odds.

Don't ever underestimate your ability to negotiate for what you want by simply outlasting someone else. If you have patience, use it. If you don't have patience, build it before you lose a negotiation.

There are ten important steps that make you a better negotiator. Believe me—we must use these ten amazing steps to make a billion dollars. It doesn't have to be millions or billions; it could be thousands of hundreds. I call them proposals. Your proposals are what you offer to the other person. A negotiation is a series of exchanges where one person offers a proposal, and the other person counterproposes. The structure of your proposals can spell success or lead to disaster. Don't let another person counterpropose on you, because you automatically lose the deal and can lose thousands of dollars.

Step One: Be Confident

When you negotiate, confidence is a great attribute to help you to win. A great deal begins in confidence. When you have deep confidence, your counterpart usually recognizes the confidence that you exude. That makes you a better negotiator. Don't overestimate your counterpart, because you can end up losing time, money, and your life.

Thinking with confidence is a form of positivity. I used to say, "I will be a billionaire," and now I say, "How can I be confident and become a billionaire?"

First, never stop dreaming. When god sent me into this great world, I had a vision to be a great man. Believe it or not, my first phrase was, "I'm too big to fail." I have a dream to pursue and things to accomplish in order make my dream come true.

I will give you my keys to success and reveal how I became a billionaire. There are six rules to being confident.

I recall the first time I made a speech in front of an audience, while I was still at Liberty High School. My legs were shaking, and my heart pounded. My brain kept shouting that I could not do it, and I could not drag myself to the stage. I was really lost until my professor told me that if I did not get up on stage, he'd fail me. I marched toward the stage and delivered my presentation without any problems. When my speech was done, I knew I was meant to talk to big crowds. My confidence level had increased.

In business, there will always be times when we're forced to step out of our comfort zones, and to appear good while doing so. If you struggle with self-confidence in your company, here are six tips that will help.

1. Keep learning.

Learning about your business will do wonders. Always be aware of seminars and courses that can keep you up-to-date on your industry or make you more in the know regarding business overall. What will happen if you don't update your memory? My first business in the United States failed. I was confident about getting a food truck, but I never researched how to run a food truck business. I failed by not learning about my activism.

2. Have a clear vision.

My vision was to get the food truck and make a lot of money. But that was not the case. One method to improve your confidence is to establish objectives. By having a concise vision of what you want your business to become, you will be in an improved position to work toward that goal. Do not make goals that are overly broad, such as "I want to make a lot of money." Instead, aim toward something like "I want to add three new customers a month," or "I want to see a rise in my search each week." As you establish measurable objectives, it is possible to view your progress. Also, it will make you more confident.

Step Two: Become Optimistic

In 2016, when candidates running for the presidency of United State of America, my mentor was the last man standing and won. On my first day in America, I went to a library and bought his great book. That day I became an optimist. I had more dreams and saw myself different than others because I learned his foundation. I always think positively in business, even if I'm failing, because optimism is thinking positively. Negativity can reduce your motivation and drag you down. As we surround ourselves with good energy, we are automatically more productive. Have a powerful group of positive influences around you who'll support your goals. Not only are they able to provide you a little push when you are feeling sluggish, but they're also able to reel you in when you get off track.

Step Three: Take a Risk

Helen Keller once said, "Life either is nothing at all or an adventure." Some will approvingly nod their heads, and others are a lot more comfortable doing what they have always done. Someplace in the middle is the knowledge that making progress requires being open to new technology, ideas, and occasionally fresh environments. These methods of doing things temporarily remove us from our comfort zones, and they often lead to great things. If a concept needs the experience of others, we should always be open to reaching out to those who can help. I frequently rely on people who follow me on Twitter and Facebook to advise me about issues or steer me toward useful connections.

5. Ditch doubt.

If you possess good ideas, but a phobia of moving ahead has you paralyzed, take it step by step. Many times we'll blame the lack of knowledge, funds, and support, when in fact we're blocking our road to success. Do not listen to negativity; have faith. You may be shocked at what you're able to achieve.

6. Recognize small things you have accomplished.

When you make that initial sale, celebrate. As you diffuse a problem that might have exploded out of control, give yourself a pat on your back. Those little victories will serve as a reminder of how talented you are and that you have more business successes to go.

Others may assist you on your path to self-confidence, but ultimately it is up to you. Following the above steps will guide you toward what you need to improve your business, and to prove to yourself that you are able and prepared to excel.

Step Four: Be Polite

Being polite is a matter of etiquette; it's about respect and being considerate of people's feelings, culture, and values. It does not seem difficult, but for many people, it remains a challenge. Some people have no interest in politesse. If you're reading this, you're probably wondering how you can improve your etiquette. At the very least, you might want to know how to avoid being rude or boorish, which can put off the people around you. Being polite is also a good way to make friends.

The only way to win a business is by being polite, and the one who introduces himself first will be the winner. Introduce yourself first. Don't wait until your opponent introduces himself or herself, because you will lose the negotiation. Being respectful gives you an efficient business and life. I use politeness like a strategy. If you introduce yourself before your opponent, you will have more advantage than your buyer or seller. Being respectful is one of the keys to making the best deal in your life. Believe me—it's fun. I made a deal for a food truck, but I'm not beginning with only money. I'm also making friends, and in the future, I'll make more money than any other because everybody trusts me. I have friends across the world, and that makes it easy to drive a better financial deal. In negotiations, girls are so intelligent because of their attractiveness. But remember when you face this situation, don't let her attract your eyes, because you will lose a perfect negotiation. Think that you're dealing with a beast because that is how they are. Don't overestimate them, even if it's your family, because in business everyone wants to win, and you will be a loser. Be peaceful all the time, but don't give your opponent chances to bite you, because she or he will bite you hard.

Negotiate without pressuring.

Do it without pressuring the people around you and making them feel like they're being pushed into a corner. For example, if you're having a conversation, it's one thing to ask a question or offer your opinion, but it's rude to push the matter when someone has verbally or nonverbally expressed discomfort about the subject. Even if you're trying to help, like offering to pay for lunch or wash the dishes, don't be too insistent. If the person says, "No, thank you, I've got it," then say, "Please? I'd really love to help." If they still say no, then let it go. They obviously want to treat you, so let them do so, and return the favor some other time. Before you act, think twice, because that will you make a better person.

Step Five: Don't Be Nervous

Business requires valor because everybody wants to take advantage of you. Don't ever be nervous about asking advice. Use to be nervous to ask advice to develop my knowledge. Is so important to update your information, skills because by update your information you may win and win. On food truck, you must research much information about food, location, and customer needs. Besides the information, you will provide a better service to your customer.

I fell in business because of my ignorance to ask advice to an old man who involved in food truck business. I went and took a food truck, without information or advice that the food truck will be not an easy business to manage. Is like your walking blind on the world. I was so excited to run my first business in United State but that was an illusion, Enthusiastic, eager, excited.

Step Six: Make Eye Contact

It's important to have eye contact, or else you will lose a negotiation. In our first post in this two-part series on eye contact, we discussed the importance of eye contact and some of the reasons we don't always feel comfortable looking someone in the eye. But just because eye contact is a great thing and a vital tool for improving the quality of all your face-to-face interactions with others, that doesn't mean that more eye contact is always better, or that all eye contact is created equal. You must do it at the right time and in the right way. That is what we'll be exploring today. We'll start off with a primer on how to make good eye contact in general conversational situations, and then we'll tackle eye contact tips for specific scenarios. Let's get started.

Eye contact can give away what you're thinking and how you're feeling. Managing your eye contact is a skill all leaders need to master. It's is the most immediate and noticeable nonverbal message you can send others. Not enough eye contact, and people deem you untrustworthy. Too much eye contact may seem inappropriate for most professional settings. But how do you know how much eye contact is too little or too much? And where do you actually look when you're looking someone in the eye? According to Sayler, the appropriate amount of eye contact should be "a series of long glances instead of intense stares." Below are a few other etiquette rules about eye contact you should keep in mind:

Eye contact with a business associate. This positioning is most appropriate in a business situation. Imagine a line below your business associate's eyes. This will serve as the base of a triangle, and the peak will be at the mid-forehead. To maintain a professional contact, keep your eyes in the middle of that triangle when speaking to others.

Eye contact in a personal relationship. If you know the other person on a personal level, invert the triangle so that its peak is now at the mouth. Still keep your eyes focused in the middle of the triangle, which is now at the tip of their nose. Also, be aware that spending too much time looking at the lower half of someone's face may give off inappropriate nonverbal messages.

Eye contact with controlled blinking. "We tend to blink more when we are under stress, so learn to control your blink rate," Sayler says. If you're trying to send a serious message, you should practice your direct eye contact without blinking, because "limited blinking adds to your message's credibility."

Managing your eye contact is important because it can give away what you're thinking and how you're feeling. In a business environment, you need to learn how to monitor your own eye contact and movements. These messages are the most expressive of all nonverbal messages.

When thinking about eye contact, you should also be aware of the cultures involved. Direct and prolonged eye contact is seen as a sign of trustworthiness and is more appreciated in Western cultures. On the other hand, it may be seen as a sign of disrespect to look directly at a superior in Eastern cultures.

Step Seven: Be Funny

Humor is criticism cloaked as entertainment and directed at a specific target, such as a negotiation. A humor target can be almost anything or anybody, but you need to be sure you've focused on the right target for your negotiation. Humor is an attempt to challenge the status quo, but targeting must reaffirm the audiences or any type of business hostilities and prejudices. Successful humorists select targets with universal appeal.

A sense of humor gives you unique attractiveness and professionalism, fostering a good relationship. In business you can attract more people: investors, bankers, and politicos. The surprise is one of the primary reasons why people laugh. It's no wonder, then, that it's also one of the primary building blocks for a successful business. Humor in business gives you the advantage to convince the buyer who wants to invest in your plan or project. Humor gives you motivation, and everything will become positive. Even when you're losing money or a negotiation, you will find a solution to your problem because you always stay positive by being happy.

A key to success is by having a sense of humor. President Dwight D. Eisenhower said, "A sense of humor is part of the art of leadership, of getting along with people, of getting things done." When I bought the food truck, I always had fun, even though I lost money. It reminds me that I'm fighting for something that I believe, fighting for my dreams. But remember that you have to pay a price for what you believe is right for you.

Step Eight: Ask Questions

Believe it or not, by asking a question, you will be more competitive. Probably your plans or ideas will work in a way that you never imagined. It's not just about business—it can be in love, school, or career. In love, for a good relationship, you must ask a question in order for the couple to enjoy the time together. If you love your wife or girlfriend, you have to ask questions about what they believe, in order to understand each other.

Communication gives you certain rules to follow in order to persuade your dream and achieve it with your wife or girlfriend. In school, you should ask many questions, especially when you don't understand the subject. In business, the art of asking questions is a recipe for success.

How well do you ask questions?

From my experience, most managers don't think about this issue. After all, you don't usually find "the ability to ask questions" on any list of managerial competencies. Neither is it an explicit part of the curriculum of business schools or executive education programs. But asking questions effectively is a major underlying part of a manager's job, which suggests that it might be worth giving this skill a little more focus. Applying it in business gives a determination of success or determination.

We've all experienced times when we've failed at being good questioners, perhaps without realizing it. For example, not long ago I sat in on a meeting where a project team was reviewing its progress with a senior executive sponsor. During the presentation, it was clear from his body language that the executive was uncomfortable with the direction the team was taking. As a result, without any real questioning of the team, he deferred approval of the next steps until he could have further discussion with the team leader. When he met with the team leader later, he ripped into him for allowing the team to go off course. Eventually, the team leader explained the thinking behind the plan, convinced the executive that they would indeed achieve their objectives, and was given the go-ahead. But in the meantime, the team had lost its momentum (and a week of productivity), and it began to focus more on pleasing the sponsor rather than doing the project in the best way.

Step Nine: Be Ready to Walk Away

You know what your break-even point is, and you know if that's not what you're getting. Be willing to walk out the door if that's the case. You might find that the other party will call you back, but you should feel happy with your efforts if they don't. You don't always get what you want, but remember that's how business works. When I was searching for companies that sold food trucks, not all of them gave me a result that I wanted. Be ready to walk away and make a good statement. This is how I do business, and I made pennies until I could make billions.

When I'm dealing with a businessman, I always try to predict what he is thinking about me. By that ideology, I consider what I have to do to get him. Many people realize less than optimal results during negotiations because they allow themselves to be dominated by fear. In order to optimize your success in any negotiation, you must be ready and willing to walk away. This doesn't necessarily mean that you actually walk away—only that you are comfortable doing so. The key is not being too attached to any particular outcome.

This attitude applies to almost all business situations. Let's say that the seller is asking for $1,000,000 for the business. You believe that you should pay no more than $750,000. The current owner is stubborn, yet you really want the business and don't want to sabotage the deal. Being attached to buying the business on the seller's terms can cost you a great deal of extra money. If you feel that it is in your best interests to pay no more than

$750,000, the wisest financial and emotional decision you can make is to offer this amount and be willing to walk away without any worry or regret.

This simple act of not worrying about the outcome will, more often than not, work to your advantage. The truth of the matter is that most people are worriers, and it is very likely that the person you are in negotiations with is one of them. Although there are some exceptions, the seller is unlikely to slam the door on the deal at this point. He or she can turn you down, but there is a definite downside to this approach, because turning down a sure thing for a potential unknown.

A counteroffer is likely, and if the seller knows that you are willing to walk away, the counteroffer is likely to be much lower than if he senses your fear. This is pretty basic stuff. The key to success in any negotiation is the absolute willingness to walk away with no regrets. You can implement this approach with the utmost respect for individuals with whom you are negotiating. There is never a need, and certainly never any advantage, to being aggressive or obnoxious. All you need is a worry-free attitude. I encourage you to try this strategy in both your current and future negotiations. I have the utmost confidence that you will appreciate the results.

The best deal.

The best deal in my life was when I decided to buy the trailer, and I found it at a good price. When you make a deal, don't let your emotions interfere with your deal. Don't let the negotiation process intimidate you. The worst that can happen is you hear no. Let me show you how to make the best deal and make billions. Any object is made by a deal, but how can you make it better? Negotiating is a part of everyday life, whether or not we notice it. Sometimes negotiations are as simple as coming to a consensus on dinner plans; others are more involved and lead to lower prices and better value on big-ticket purchases. From credit card rates to home improvement projects, from cars to houses, consumers should assume everything is open to negotiation, especially in a slowly recovering economy.

Anything that we buy is a deal.

How do you make a deal in love? Find someone who gives you motivation, either women or man. Don't ever think about getting married without a proposal to your love. In business, sex is a form that we use to satisfy our neediness. In these days, love doesn't exist. Loves lie. People say that if you are married, you have to use a certain process to secure your life from disaster. My friend was a billionaire and owned ranches, private chalets, houses, and many others things. He asked me for advice about what he should do to avoid problems with his future love. I said, "Before you get married, you have to make a proposal to your future wife."

We human beings let our emotions drive our future. My friend didn't listen to my advice, and he was happy for a couple of months. I remember one day I was in my office, discussing a deal for the food trailer, and I heard the phone ring. Guess who it was? My friend—without a wife and a happy life. His wife divorced him and took 75 percent of his wealth.

This does not happen only to my friend. It happened to my mentor, President Donald J. Trump. Donald Trump handles it with a prenup, but I call it a proposal. President Trump has been married to his third wife, Melania Knauss, since 2005. His first marriage to Ivana Zelnickova lasted from 1977 to 1992, reportedly ending in a $25 million settlement for Ivana. He was married to his second wife, Marla Maples, from 1993 to 1999. That's how he made a mistake, just like my friend. It can happen to you too. But thanks to him, we can prevent this disaster and live happily with our wives. Believe me, you will save a lot of money, and in the end you'll thank me.

First: If she won't sign a prenup, she's not the wife for you.

If she won't sing a prenup or proposal, it means she does not love you—she loves your money. The most difficult aspect of the prenuptial agreement is informing your future spouse, "I love you very much, but just in case things don't work out, this is what you will get in the divorce: 0 percent."

There are basically three types of women and reactions. One is the good woman who very much loves her future husband, solely for himself, but refuses to sign the agreement on principle. I fully understand this, but the man should take a pass anyway and find someone else. The other is the calculating woman who refuses to sign the prenuptial agreement because she is expecting to take advantage of the poor, unsuspecting sucker she's got in her grasp. There is also the woman who will openly and quickly sign a prenuptial agreement in order to make a quick hit and take the money given to her. (Trump, *The Art of the Comeback*)

If they don't want to sign your proposal, find another. This world is full of men and women who are sexier than the one that you used to have. Sometimes this used to happen to me but, no longer. The attractiveness kills you quick. Think about this: a hot, sexy women wants to meet you. Without having time to meet her, you will say yes. Because she's hot, you're willing to do anything, but that makes you a loser, so stay away from that.

Second: To avoid disagreements, simply tell your wife what to do.

By telling your wife what to do, both of you will achieve more success and make a lot of money. In the family, someone needs to lead, because we need a person to show the ways to achieve our dreams. Just like any president who leads a country, we select a person to run our country, economy, and security because we want things done well. You have to be in charge. Don't let your wife or girlfriend lead your future.

Third: Don't make the mistake of giving your wife business responsibilities.

My big mistake with Ivana was taking her out of the role of wife and allowing her to run one of my casinos in Atlantic City, then the Plaza Hotel. The problem was, work was all she wanted to talk about. When I got home at night, rather than talking about the softer subjects of life, she wanted to tell me how well the Plaza was doing, or what a great day the casino had. I really appreciated all her efforts, but it was just too much. I will never again give a wife responsibility within my business. Ivana worked very hard, and I appreciated the effort, but I soon began to realize that I was married to a businessperson rather than a wife.

In my case, I will never marry because a wife wants to enroll in my business. Businesswomen marry because they see the best deal to secure their future. I decide to be single because nobody will make a decision about what I have to do. If I want to have kids, I will pay someone to have my kids and raise them the way I want. If I want to send my kids to a business school in London, I don't have to disagree or agree with my wife, because she doesn't exist. I know I'm doing the right thing for my kids. I have to lead them and make them billionaires.

Everyone wants to be a billionaire, but I want my kids to be trillionaires. Just like me, they should have the ambition to become trillionaires. I don't share the same ambition as President Trump, Bill Gates, Warren Buffett, Jack Ma, Barack Obama, George W. Bush, Putin, or my great mentor John D. Rockefeller. I'm too big to fail. Even though I'm still small, I have faith in success. Beyond a deal, you have to know how to close it. I never let someone make decisions for me because I'm driving my future, and I want it great. Don't let your spouse, your parent, or anybody drive your life. You have the key to become a success, not them.

Trust your odds.

Getting customers, clients, and employees to trust you can be complicated, but it is imperative for success, perhaps even more important than sales. If you get others to trust you, it's easier to grow your business and give everyone excellent service. But trust is fragile. If you lose it, it's very difficult, if not impossible, to restore it.

In this world, it's not easy to start a business, but it's not impossible. Five years ago, I tried to be in the marketing system. Everybody rejected me because of my age, language, and skills. For once in my life, I was ready to paint and make a lot of money. Everybody rejected me because they didn't consider me a businessman. They considered me a fake person.

Nobody considers me a young visionary because I don't have a characteristic that they require to accomplish their dreams and make them rich. I decided to build mine on an empire. If you tell people that you are a businessman, they will reject you because they know you may destroy them. But if you tell them to hire you, they will because you're helping them to build their dreams.

Remember that when you're working for any company that doesn't bellow to you, you are living another person's dreams. But we can make a better business than your boss.

In 2016, I invested in a small ranch that can produce meet at the high quality needed in the US market. All of the world is raising cattle in a way that doesn't allow them to make a lot of profit. I have begun researching a new way that gives me an advantage on producing meat in a short period of time. My supply can meet all of the world's demands. But when I was searching for this project, my friends, family, and others said that it was the stupidest idea they'd ever heard. I never lost my momentum, and I believe in my odds.

I worked on my project for one year until the building was done. Then I bought eight cattle to show that my project was not wrong and could help farmers quickly grow their cattle in a new way.

How to advertise any business.

It's necessary to advertise your business a few days before you open. Why? Because you will have the advantage of getting a few customers before the date that you open. Advertising has evolved into a vastly complex form of communication, with literally thousands of different ways for a business to get messages to the consumer. Today's advertiser has a vast array of choices at his or her disposal. The Internet alone provides many of these, with the advent of branded viral videos, banners, advertorials, sponsored websites, branded chat rooms, and so much more. Sometimes you must keep it a secret until you experiment with your project or any plan that you're willing to expose. If you expose any plan or project that you haven't experimented on, you will have competition that you can't compete with, and you will be out of business. With my food trailer, I never thought about how important it was to advertise a business before I tried to put it in action. I supposed I'd let my future customers discover that I sold the best food ever. But I made a big mistake, and that cost me money. That's why I wrote this book, because I don't want you to lose money. I want you to make money every single day.

Strategy

The most important foundation in business is strategy. I will share you the best strategy to help you win. You will get tired of winning. The strategy is not about being the best, but about being unique. Competing to be the best in business is one of the major misconceptions. That strategy will make you a better businessman, and it's also one of the steps to building your momentum. If you only remember one tip from this list, it should be this one. Many leaders compare competition in business with the world of sports: there can only be one winner. But competing in business is more complex. There can be several winners. It does not have to be a zero-sum game where you win and I lose, or vice versa. If your big brother wins, you also have a ticket to win because in business everybody has a chance to make it. It depends on how much effort you're willing to expend. Within a single industry, you can have several companies beating the industry average, each with a distinctive and different strategy. They are no direct threat to each other. There can be several winners. The worst possible approach to strategy is to seek out the biggest player in the industry and try to copy everything that person does. I love food, and I assume everybody does. I have many plans. One of them is my food trailer. My plan was to get a trailer and expand until I turned it into a restaurant and built a big empire.

Things will not always got how you predict. After six months, my business was ruined. I didn't have the option to rebuild, and I closed. But I did not quit. As I said, I'm too big to fail.

This is how we created the plan.

Our Business Plan

Executive

Pieanha House is the new revolution for food trucks. Our plates are the most delicious ever. We offer satisfaction, quality, freshness, and more. We started in 2015 with a vision to introduce our business in the marketing system of food trucks and restaurants.

CEO

Amadeo Vasquez is the CEO of Pieanha House. Our goal is introducing our product to the market. The CEO will form and implement the key mission of Pieanha House food truck, leading to success.

To Sum It Up

In order to be a big success in any field, you need to build momentum. Momentum is all about energy and timing. When you start anything new, you have no momentum, and that's when things are hard. People are not calling you, and you do not seem to be getting anywhere. But if you keep at it and keep working toward your goals, one day at a time, then soon you will get into the flow of people and events. You get contracts, gain credibility, and build a track record of success; things get much easier. Why? Because you have momentum.

But do not take momentum for granted. If you lose your momentum, all your success ends, and things get much more difficult. It is dangerous to do anything when you have lost your momentum. Your timing is off, and people and events are no longer in your favor. Watch out and never lose your momentum.

Company Ownership

The company will start as a simple proprietorship, owned by its founders: Tzoc Tetzaguic, Miguel, Amadeo Vasquez, and Zeit Mseke. As the company grows, the owner will consider re-registering as a limited liability company or as a corporation (International Business)—anything that will suit the future business and its needs.

Start-up

The company founders will handle day-to-day operations of the plan, and they will work collaboratively to ensure that Pieanha House's venture is a success. They estimate that the start-up costs will require money, including legal costs, advertising, and related expenses.

Additional money will be required in a bank account as operating capital for the first three months of operation. The start-up costs are to be financed in equal portions by the founders.

Partnership and Financial Invest

Partnership and financial investment require the most courageous people in the world. Amadeo Vasquez is the CEO of Pieanha House because he knows the power of thinking big and staying positive.

SIMPLE PROCESS TO BUILDING UP

Location does not matter, because we find a simple way to increase our business in a different sector. After providing a facility for our business, a new opportunity, and a facility to our customers to access to our operation, the most important thing as a corporation is the increment of profit.

The location will not affect the business because we're making a sophisticated plan that will change the way we trade. Billionaires optimize the most important and unique things that matter for a business, which is the quality of each product. In developing each business, you should optimize, understand, and make credible the costumes, but in certain ways the matter is how your idea and plan made it.

The Capital Necessary for Starting Pieanha House Food Truck Business

We know that the entire payment is up to $27,000, not specifying the extra expenses that must be covered. Also, we know how much money we need, and it depends on how our strong plan is. In a simple way for opening small, it will be approximately $10,000–15,000 just to start a business.

Let's start with this little math practice for how much we invest and how much we'll get back.

Local Competitors

Competitive analysis conducted by the company founders have shown that 26,000 companies currently offer some sort of food corner service in the Houston, Texas, area. However, most of the incumbent competitors offer only a limited line of services. In fact, of these 26,000 competitors, only five offered a range of food corner services comparable with the options that Pieanha House plans to offer all the United States.

Personnel Plan

Initially, Pieanha House's personal food plan will include only the founders, and they will arrange the food truck. As the personnel plan shows, the founders are expected to hire additional workers in the next year. The management decisions will be controlled by the founders and some hired managers.

Summary

With Pieanha House's extensive experience in the field and the commitment to provide profitable food corner, the company will grow and is certain that it will capture the necessary market share to achieve its financial goals. Armed with a competitive spirit and a genuine love for its clients and workers, Pieanha House is eager to serve the United States of America, starting with Houston, to plan the most delicious meals in the market for many years to come.

Get Out Expired Items

I think running a business, doing what I've done for the last—since 1996, has taught me so many things because I started from just an idea and then had to figure out how to make it, market it, every single thing from soup to nuts on how to get a product done and out there.
—Lori Greiner

Selling a product sounds easy. Keep in mind that it is not. My landlord told me that she works two jobs, and I was shocked. She has three properties, and they all have businesses, shops, and offices for rent. She has three corner stores. After all that, she still tells me that she is going to open four gas stations. That was fascinating. She gave us a good deal for parking our food truck. In our food truck, we had all of the products we needed to cook the recipes. For the first two months, we lost all the food that could be sold for one month. Well, that is business. We had a list of everything that was in the food truck. Every day before we start selling food, we check the list. We make sure everything that we need is there. Having surprises when cooking is not uplifting. When you are planning to sell perishable items, then you must have a list to check if the dates have passed. Try to update it every day, if possible.

DEAL WITH CONTRACTORS

Contractors will first want to sell you on the deal. You bring yourself to the contractor, yet you get the bad deal. Negotiating skills is the beating heart of dealing with contractors. Tzoc has dealt with a lot of contractors. He had to deal with them in his business of painting. Ninety percent of the time, people end up agreeing with a contractor. Why do they get to agree? People usually don't like to work hard and go all around looking for different contractors. When getting a location, you mast work hard enough to get the deal that you want. If you are looking for a deal of 60 percent out of 100 percent, then go get it. Tzoc and I went shopping for locations. Everywhere we went, the contractor told us that we had to pay $1,300 to put the food truck there. That was a lot of money considering the situation we were in, and the deal we were looking for was $700–1,000. Searching for a location is really hard. Those who say it is easy end up getting a location that is not good for the business. The location that doesn't produce profit is a location far away from customers. For some people, it is easy because businesses differ. If you are opening a restaurant, cafe spot, shop, clinic, insurance company, or any work in businesses, then you need to be close to your customers. Those who say it is easy are those from the Internet age. These people don't meet with customers, and if they do meet, they meet customers at a café spot, at the customer's complex, at the seller's complex, or at a library. These people sell beauty products, electronics, athletic clothes, jewelry, and office supplies.

MAKING EXCELLENT DECISIONS IN BUSINESS AND IN FUTURE LIFE

Making excellent decisions is crucial in business and in life. You can choose a career, you can choose a low-paying job, or you can choose to have a business of your own, being the boss of others. All that is there for you to choose. If your life, people have been making decisions for you. Now it is time to transform. Suggestions are okay if you get to make the decision in the end. Family members like to suggest most things. You should go to this college, you should go to this university, you should take this career path, you should marry this type of a person—it never ends. They keep influencing your days for bad or for good. You hear friends all the time say, "You should come with us." They know how to please with words.

Look around you. I know you see something that you can change in your life today. Perhaps you have taken that first step. Keep moving to the next steps. Transform how you talk about yourself and your interests to reflect you, not others. Your contribution to others means contributing to yourself, your approach in people you deal with day to day, your obligations, your behaviors, and lastly your way of managing money.

People frequently fail to define freedom, devotion, and being financially free. When you understand those words, particularly *freedom*, you can open your eyes. Do you want to be working your entire life? Do you want be told what to do? Would you like to be free from your restraints and accomplish your dreams? Would you like to travel the other sides of the world? Would you like to be financially free? Then think about these three phrases carefully.

Freedom + Devotion + Financially Free

Definition of Freedom

The quality or state of being free; the power to do what you want
to do; the absence of necessity, coercion, or constraint in choice or
action; liberty from slavery or restraint or from the power of another.

In this world, you have a dream that you want to achieve. Have the power
to do what you want. A person who works for other people's dreams has
no way to achieve his or her own dream for success. It is understandable
that the meaning for success is different for deferent people. Remember
that those who do not work hard for their dreams end up working hard to
make other people be financially free. Seek the freedom from negativity
and necessity, and have the power to do what you love. That is a freedom
worth achieving. Keep moving forward and stay true to yourself.

Definition of Devotion

A feeling of strong love or loyalty; the use of time,
money, energy, etc., for a particular purpose.

Have a purpose in your life. Be the ruler of your mountains. Stand strong.
Being able to manage your many is very important. When you have
energy to do something, do it. You must save your money for something
greater. Be the light of your life. Keep your mind straightforward. Don't
let difficulty stand on your way. Get out of your dark world and start living
in to the light.

Definition of Financially Free

The state of having sufficient personal wealth to live,
without having to work actively for necessities.

When you think about financial freedom, what do you think about? What
do you feel in you? What must you do to achieve that freedom? Everyone
has the desire to be financially free. Being financially free gives you more
free time than you need. Working hard for two to four years is what you
must do. You must keep your life motivated. Every day you wake up, you

must have the trust that you are getting there. There will be difficulties, but remember that they must not be the objective of your life. Live to fight all your problems in life. Get to retirement for better or for worse. If you are already over fifty years old, you still have a chance to achieve all your dreams. Don't let your daily life complicate you dream to be financially free. Tzoc always talks about doing things just after the evaluation of the good and bad things about that idea. He always says, "Let's start." We sleep only three hours and then do things that we consider worth achieving. Today, start working for your dreams.

Excellent Decision Quotes

Challenges meet everyone in this world. No matter how secure people are, they can fall down and get up again. When they get up, they realize the lesson they just learned from falling down is the most breathtaking lesson in their lives. When you fall down, it does not mean that you must quit working for what you have been seeking you entire life. Stand tall for that idea. Guard that idea. Integrate it within you. A few people have not accepted falling down. However, when they fall down, they make sure that they get up again. They can't get up without making the right decision from their failures and past decisions. The following quotes are great to refresh your brain now and then.

> "When defeat comes, accept it as a signal that your plans are not sound, rebuild those plans, and set sail once more toward your coveted goal. If you give up before your goal has been reached, you are a 'quitter.' A quitter never wins, and a winner never quits."
> —Napoleon Hill

> "Part of being a winner is knowing when enough is enough. Sometimes you have to give up the fight and walk away. Move on to something else that's more productive."
> —Donald Trump

"I get up at 4 o'clock in the morning, I'm usually in the office by 5–5:30am. You know people always complain to me about traffic in Toronto and how bad it is, and I say when I go to the office there's no traffic."
—Robert Herjavec

"When I had challenges, it taught me to be more on top of it for the future. Things go wrong all the time when you're running your own business, but it's how you perceive it and deal with it that matters."
—Lori Greiner

"I bought a company in the mid-'90s called Dexter Shoe and paid $400 million for it. And it went to zero. And I gave about $400 million worth of Berkshire stock, which is probably now worth $400 billion. But I've made lots of dumb decisions. That's part of the game."
—Warren Buffett

"It doesn't matter how many times you have failed, you only have to be right once."
—Mark Cuban

"Doing the best at this moment puts you in the best place for the next moment."
—Oprah Winfrey

"Without the ability to visualize a goal and believe it will be reached, nothing of substance will be achieved. Not by anybody. Not at any time. Not in any place."
—Robert Herjavec

"I've been making products for so long, I have a gut feel for what is right—what will work and what won't. I can tell instantly if it's a hero or a zero."
—Lori Greiner

"There is only one boss. The customer. And he can fire everybody in the company from the chairman on down, simply by spending his money somewhere else."
—Alice Walton

"If you can't make it good, at least make it look good."
—Bill Gates

"I had no idea that being your authentic self could make me as rich as I've become. If I had, I'd have done it a lot earlier."
—Oprah Winfrey

Never give up. Today is hard, tomorrow will be worse, but the day after tomorrow will be sunshine.
—Jack Ma

The Voyage Is for Oneself

It is all about you. You must know that it is time for you to change. Change your path. make a choice that will lighten your road to success. Success is hard, but hard is worth achieving. You need to have a road that is lit. With a lit road, you can see the path you are taking on your journey to success. Stay strong, stay on time, and stay on date. Accomplish all your steps in business. Be the temple of your soul. Stand strong. Don't let anyone stand in front of you with worthless words, like "you are not strong," "you are going the wrong way," "you are not going to succeed," "you are nothing if you don't do this," and "you will lose." You should automatically delete these people. If you can help them see the light you have sought, then help them. Don't let those people take away your time. Your schedule matters more than other people's schedule. If you can attend to their need of you, then you have to go, but if you can't attend, then you don't. Tell them you are in something. You must come first before others. Don't let them stand in front of your achievements. Be you. Stand with light. Lighten your business and put yourself into it. Mix yourself into your dream. Submit yourself to it, and you will make it. If you are mixed into your dream, then you became the dream. The dream and you are one. Success becomes like changing a light bulb. Success is just the beginning.

No one was born with a bloodline of success. Some people will say, "You were never born to be a success. You were born to work for us. You are miserable." I have been planning to let you know that how you grow and the people around you are the key points that shape your view of the world. Those people in your life will pave some of your road to success, and it is bumpy. Remember when you were young, and your mother had to take you to a playground to play? Well, when you were there for your fist time, you had to learn how to use the playground equipment. That is how business is; knowledge is the key.

Be aware of the bad ones around you. They are not truly bad; they simply have a different view than you. You see the success of your life and business in front of you. They keep saying it is not closer, or it is not worthy to fight for. They say you will never succeed in your goals and dreams. Those people are not you. You are different for a purpose. You are strong and are the beating heart of your success. Remember that fear will keep you paralyzed in the same low income that you have right now. Stand strong. If you feel that it is taking too long for you to earn money, stop working for that company. Stop working for other people and stand up yourself; start a business. Make the right choice before moving to the next steps.

Fear that you can't make it is always there. You are a human being; it is deep down in the inner cells of your brain. That signal is in there, and it can only be taken out by you. You are the key to your situations. You are the key to your debt. You are the key to making your dreams come true, and you are the one who has key to the cave in which you are right now. It's a cave of fear and of submitting yourself to other people's ideas. Stand strong. You will work your entire life with nothing made by your name. Paint your name for your history. Don't disappear in the air like ashes. You can't get out of that cave until you see how powerful you are. Before you see how powerful you are, you have to first accept that you are powerful, not powerless. Powerless should pass in your right ear and exit the left ear. Have awareness of what surrounds you. You have to recognize the difference between you making your own decision and another person making decisions for you. What do you want the most? If you want other people making decisions for you, that weakens you in this world of economics. If you like making your own decisions, then be stronger and straightforward. Your achievements are made to be multiplied, not subtracted.

Be Careful of Emotion

Emotions sometimes put us in danger of making the decision of a lifetime. You don't want to die while having nothing of your own. Years pass so quickly. You do not like to have flashbacks of "What have I done in my life? Oh, I was living other people's successes. I was not living my success. I used my time for others." That is depressing, as you can imagine.

How do you know whether the choice you are making is not against you? Emotion plays a part in it. Remember that facts are the key to making sure you make the right choice. How did you grow up? What do your family members want you to become? What do *you* want to become? What do you think you can do until you die? These decisions that you are making come from your environment. Your environment is everyone around you because you were born on this planet. Check people you knew since you were young, and you will not see a lot of difference. When you see that, then make your decision. What do you want to do and live for?

Desire

A strong feeling of wanting to have something, or
wishing for something to happen; to long or hope for; a
usually formal request or petition for some action.

What do you want to do and live for? That question should be answered by your most strong desire. Your desire to own a business, your desire to exceed limitations, your desire to have a good revenue, your desire to live freely from following others accomplishing their dreams, your desire to live your true dream, your desire to help others on your way to the top—these can be achieved. When you are longing for something to which you do not have right now, work hard and follow your dreams. You have to work hard to achieve that one step that will bring other steps. Once you know what to do with your life, between working for others or working for yourself, take evasive action. When you make that decision, be absolute and strong. Going back to your old life should not be an option. Going back should not exist. Moving forward must be your promise to yourself. Don't let families, friends, and others who influence you or change your promise to success and win your goals. Even if you are failing the game of business, make sure to rethink your game plan. Failure must not be an option. Continue playing the game. Ask for help here and there. Do not back down. Don't be the worker—be the owner. Stand strong. Find people who share the same desires you have and then start to move step by step with that group.

Excellent Decision Is the Key to Success. Making a decision for today will affect tomorrow and the months to come. Taking correct measures step by step to extract understanding of any thought or idea that needs attention is central to excellent decision making. There are many forms of management in business. When it is the first time leading a business, the leader is energized with what he or she encounters for the first time. He or she finds greater situations to entertain. Curiosity drives a person from foolishness to awareness. For the first time, you get to manage your own business finances, marketing, strategies, operations, production, or services, and it is electrifying. Being the boss of your business is not stress-free, especially the management part. You have to keep up with your managers to make sure that all the organizing and managing is running smooth. The management part has to improve with every day that goes by. The business can meet its aims with a future achievement.

Ensure Great Decisions Are Finalized, Not Ruthless Decisions. Ruthless decisions will lead the business into catastrophe. You are in business to win today, to win tomorrow, and to win in the months ahead. I know you are a winner. You are a lion chaser. Great decisions are where you must focus your attention. Having a checklist is one of the most effective ways to do that. Make yourself a day-to-day checklist. Each day, you must check your list with all the accomplishments that you achieve. Keep track of that checklist and make sure you follow it. Most people get frustrated with questions when they are not sure whether they answered it right. It is normal for people to get a little out of line now and then.

The steps you are about to read here are key to making the right decision. After reading the steps, check the list that I have made. You can use this as an example, but you must make your own list after reading this book. Some people ask themselves, "What choices do I have in my thoughts or ideas? What evidence do I have that I am taking the right choice? What if the thought is difficult—what do I do next?" Those are some of the questions when making a right decision. Here are the steps to making an excellent decision in business.

Step One: Write your ideas in a notebook.

Step Two: Investigate the good and the bad of each idea.

Step Three: Bring your ideas from a high number to two ideas. Then get another point of view on the two ideas from a person whom you trust.

Step Four: Select the greater idea between those two ideas, and set that one golden idea into motion.

Your desire can be achieved. When you are longing for something to which you do not have right now, and you feel you can live doing it for your entire life, then don't waste your time. Take evasive action. When you make that decision, please be sure and clear. You must have a great quality for uniqueness. Aristotle once said, "Quality is not an act, it is a habit." Do your best. Do not go back—move forward. Even if you are losing the game, try to rethink your game plan so that you can continue to play.

STAY POSITIVE AND ACTIVE THROUGH YOUR HARDSHIP VOYAGE OF BUSINESS

Staying positive and active is the way to ride the roller coaster of business. You will experience hard days, hard weeks, and hard months. Remember that those hard days are the most uplifting days of your life in business. You tumble two or three times before you can start walking. In business, it is the same principle. There is no such thing as "start today, get rich tomorrow." Those are children's stories. Starting from the bottom is the best way to start. We always learn from our mistakes, even if the mistakes are minor. We learn something from it.

One of my close friends in Africa tumbled from having millions of dollars to having pennies. That is not a good ride on the roller coaster, but he made it in the end. His name is Wika Tukundana. He was twenty-two years old when his father died. When his father died, he was faced with a lot of responsibility. He had to take care of all his family's businesses and land, as well as his two sisters, Emily Tukundana and Layla Tukundana, and his mother, Chantelle Tukundana. His father was a courageous, strong man. He was loyal to customers and respected the dignity and opinions of others. His father owned two small markets in Bwiza, Burundi. Both markets had the same name: Tukunda Duka. The land of the two markets and the land where the Tukundana family house was constructed were owned by his father. His father died and had already built a fortune for his family.

The day-to-day business responsibilities fell to Wika Tukundana. He was the older brother. He was a little bit different from his father. He went to college parties, was a dancing fanatic, hung out with friends, was a soccer player, and was devoted to baking bread. Anything that dealt with baking, he was on it. He enjoyed baking bread, and so we named him Mr. Bread. His big sister was attending university, and his younger sister was attending private high school. They were moving well with every corner of the roller coaster when his father was alive. Wika took control of the business and the Tukundana house's tasks. Wika was a year away from finishing his university path. He had to withdraw from university and start taking responsibility of the business that his father had. That was not a moral choice, particularly when he was only a year from graduating. He started taking care of the business tasks, raising his sisters, keeping his mother in health, and taking care of his intolerable feeling of nearly graduating. Wika treasured his sisters. If you love your sisters in a way that you don't want to let go, you always try to look out for them. Where are they going? What time? How are they doing? Keep checking up time after time. He was good at that.

Four months after his father passed away, his mother passed away too. Wika became the sole head of the family. Support that his beloved mother used to offer vanished. Chantelle, his mother, used to support him with the necessities of running the businesses that they had. He ensured development and financial successes for the business for a couple of months. Bella, the younger sister, graduated from high school, and then difficulties started to show. Money situations started to arise. He had promised his father that he would keep his sisters in education until they finished their university education. He was not good at budgeting and financial spreadsheets. He tried to figure out where the money was going and how to get customers the way his father used to do it. The enthralling thing was that the breads that used to be sold in the Tukunda Duka markets used to be baked cooked by him. Wika used to bake them at home.

One grave night came, and he decided to sell one of the Tukunda Duka markets. He did that in order to pay tuition for Bella to start college. It was hard for Wika to make that conclusion. He told me, "My father always said to me that education is the key to unlocking opportunities with a better view of seeing the world economy. That is why I decided to send my sister to a college. I decided to take the risk and sell one of the family markets so that my sister could go to college." That was great. But then, he didn't foresee that it would not be easy to get money for daily expanses. He was not expanding the business. He was breaking the empire that his father had built.

After eight month of operating the one Tukunda Duka market that remained, he starting undergoing the downfall of the business roller coaster. Another market opened nearby, and most customers started going to the other market for their products. Wika started to think of ways to open another market. He was supposed to start thinking of how he could keep that one market in active. Defects became unbearable, and so he wanted to loan money to a bank to open another market. The good news was he didn't take loans. He was not good at strategies.

After two years of managing his father's business, Wika changed his mind. One day he told me, "One day, I was sitting in a bread shop, eating their bread with a fresh cup of tea that they sold there. I started looking for ways to change my direction of what I was selling." He went to the bank and got a loan to buy good baking equipment. From there, he changed the Tukunda Duka market to Kunda Bek.

Sometimes It's Good to Change the Direction to You Destination

Wika had a lot of open-minded strategies that he was going to use. From there, Wika started selling all types of baked goods: bread, cakes, cookies, pies, and pastries. He starting selling coffee and tea as well. The family bakery shop made a little profit for the family. After four month of the bakery shop being in business, customers started to line up for Kunda Bek's bakery. Wika had a strategy to put advertisements in the community of Bwiza about the bakery shop. The ads would say, "Bring your friends with you to Kunda Bek! Get two Bek's breads free!" sales skyrocketed, and he was amazed. He didn't know that strategy would work, but he went ahead and did it.

Two years after the bakery shop opened, he was able to open another bakery shop. By that time, Emily had graduate from university. She owned apartments in Burundi and Tanzania, and she was a nurse. Bella loved saving lives. Wika works harder in the bakery shop than when he was running his father's markets. He worked hard in his father's idea, but it didn't work. That was not the end, and he accepted change. He is committed to his change and doesn't excuse anything. He takes responsibility for the family and the business. Wika now has two bouncing baby girls.

If you're in business, you must be passionate about it. You must be committed to it. You must love it. Anything that you love doing will be greater than 95 percent. You will be doing well in down times and up times. Any business idea you take for success will accelerate into mountains of success. If you start a business that you love, even if you don't hit those thousands of dollars, you will be fine. You will be okay. Here is some heads-up. When someone asks you, "How are you doing in your business?" You should tell that person your business is doing great. Use positive words. Then tell that person to stop by your business. When that person is at your business, tell him or her about your business. What product or service do you offer? Tell that person your love and commitment for your success. Why is it important? What is the difference between you and your competition? After you have that short conversation about your business, I will bet that person will become a future customer. He will bring you other customers too. That is the best way to build up your first mountain and continue with others. It helps you have more motivation to stay active all day and night. That builds your openness. Be with people whom you hold dear: family members, friends, or colleagues. Tell them about your business. Remember positive words.

POSITION ENERGY TO ACCOMPLISH MORE THAN ANTICIPATED

The road that paves the way to success is the road that keeps you on track to success. Friends can be bad and good. People whom you spend time around paint your way to successor or failure. You are looking to that gold of a successor. If you are around people who keep you back, leading you from behind, they never give you a lead. They keep pushing you from the back. They always say you are not ready and will not be successful. You are never going to make it. Some people don't want you to succeed. Most of the time, they tell you about their situations. They fill you with problems of their own. They don't want to hear about your situations. They don't invest even a little time in you. Those friends are not friends. They want to keep you trapped in that rabbit cage. You have to be a brave rabbit. Everyone around you won't wish you success. If people don't want to use you, then they want to keep you down. Don't stand down. You must be strong and brave to keep on the road to success. Take the right path that has positive words, positive people, a positive attitude, and positive surroundings.

> "It's fine to celebrate success but it is more important to heed the lessons of failure."
> —Bill Gates

> "I prefer to like the people I invest in, but it's not an absolute necessity, as long as they have a good mind and I know they'll do whatever it takes to be successful."
> —Lori Greiner

"We know what we are, but know not what we may be."
—William Shakespeare

"Your work is going to fill a large part of your life, and the only way to be truly satisfied is to do what you believe is great work. And the only way to do great work is to love what you do. If you haven't found it yet, keep looking. Don't settle. As with all matters of the heart, you'll know when you find it."
—Steve Jobs

"If you can dream it, you can do it."
—Walt Disney

Surround yourself with great people who will lift you up and will work with, not against you. They make you rich with respect, and you return the favor. If the favor is not honorable, then think of a different approach. When we were negotiating for the food truck, we stumbled into bad deals that took money from us. We found two food truck companies online and one food truck company for a walk-in office. We gave them a call. The customer service is always good at first. When you want to purchase something, they can even spend five hours with you on the phone, just to sell you something.

The first company said that the food truck of the size we were looking for was $74,000. We asked them if they had one with the same size for a lower price. They said that they didn't have any for a lower price. Then we asked them to suggest a company where we could get a food truck for a lower price. The customer service refused to suggest another company. We let one day pass, and then we called again. This time we asked to speak to the manager. We waited for thirty minutes, but it was worth it. The manager came online, and her name was Katelyn. We asked the manager about the economical price compared to the luxurious price she had. She said the economical price she had was from $68,000, and the luxurious option topped out at $74,000. We asked her if she could negotiate the economical price to $60,000. Katelyn said that she'd have to speak to her boss. Then before we hung up the phone, we asked her if she could suggest a company where we could get a food truck in our price range. She said," Sure. Check this company called Food Truck of Americana. It is good for the price you are looking for."

We then called Food Truck of Americana. They were two states from us; we were in Texas by then. We asked them about their price. They told us their food trucks went from $25,000 to $100,000. That was interesting. How can a food truck cost a lot of money? I know, it is crazy. The food truck business makes good money. Check "The Seller Who Tracks the Roads to Success" in the table of contents. You will see how much food truck businesses make per month and per year. We asked them about our price range, which was $55,000– 60,000. They said they had a good deal for that price range, but they didn't have the size we needed. We skipped the Food Truck of Americana. They were far way and didn't have the size we needed.

Customer service agents don't have freedom in the company as managers do. When trying to negotiate, don't negotiate with a person lower than a manager. Keep in mind that you must respect everyone in that company if you are going to negotiate. You must give the manager full respect, you must give the other employees the same respect. You must negotiate with the manager. If you can get to negotiate the deal with the owner of the company or the item owner, you are more likely to get a good price. When you walk out of the deal, you have the information you need. You are satisfied by the results you received from the manager or the owner. Before walking out of the deal, you need to make sure you get to the owner. In the end, the owner makes the financial decision about his or her item, product, or service.

When negotiating a house or a lease for office, get straight to the landlord. He or she makes the deal more fairly. He can go below the price he or she told the manager to offer. Be very careful when making a deal that goes more than the amount you are willing to spend. Don't buy in to deals that don't work in your favor. If any deal doesn't work in your favor, you must immediately take a timeout. Go look for another two or three deals, but with different types of prices. Then try to compare the deals. Most people end up doing all that research, and they find out in the end, they took the bad deal because they took the cheapest deal. You know that cheap things don't work well. Maybe they are broken or have some other technical problems. Make sure you don't make a quick decision. Don't take the cheapest one. At the same time, don't take the expensive one that will cost you more than what you are willing to spend.

I remember in February 2017, my friend and I went to look for a car for him. His name is Dido Jagwokambe. He really needed a car because for the first time, he was moving on with his life. He was going to live by himself. Cars are very important. He and I went to CarMax and other dealers. The car that he liked was at car CarMax. He was able to afford it with the system of financing. He liked driving SUVs. All types of SUVs have four seats and must have a 4.0 or 4.5 cylinder. The hard roads of Texas are filled with holes and bumps. If you drive on this road with a small car, you may lost your investment for that small car. This roads are not like the ones in Orlando, Florida. After visiting eight different types of dealers, we went ahead and started the finance with Car Max. He was going to put $3,000 down for a 2013 Rogue Nissan. That Nissan came out at CarMax for $13,000, plus $2,000 because of financing. Government registration and taxes were $900. At CarMax, he was going to spend $15,000 total for that Nissan. Because it was financing, the amount that he was going to pay par month was $500. That is because he did not have any credit. Remember that credit is very important when it comes to finance. Dido's spending amount for a car was $5,000, and closing the deal for $7,000. The car that he was going to get at CarMax was a bad deal for Dido. Most depressing of all was that he was going to get that CarMax deal. Why did Dido want to do that? Because the features the car had and everything that he liked was in that car. He loved it too much to let go.

You should love you business like that. For businesses, sometimes we let them go. Tozc, Amadeo, and I left the food truck business. It was a hard choice, but it was worth making that choice rather than waiting to crash hard. Dido was a part-time student at Liberty High School and a part-time worker. That truck was not a great choice for him because paying $500 per month was not joke. The car was not something to play with; that is a valuable property. He used to make about $900–1,200 per month. The insurance was high. Most cars that are still like new cost a great amount of insurance. I was twenty years old at that time. CarMax said because he was financing the vehicle, he would need to get full coverage. That was interesting. When we called the insurance company to get a quote for that Nissan, we were at CarMax. Dido had the $3,000 ready to take the car. The insurance agent's name was Abigail, and she was sweet. I mean sweet with words. I was the one giving the information necessary for Abigail to fill in the information on the computer program so that we could get a quote for full coverage. When she was done, she said that the full coverage for that car was $400–700. On top of a loan of $15,900 for the car, the coverage for one year was $4,800–8,400. That was too much for the amount Dido wanted to spend. CarMax had a lot of impressive cars, but we moved to the next level.

We went to another dealer. This dealer negotiated very well. His name was Johnny, and he showed us different types of cars that he was selling. Dido told Johnny the price that he was willing to pay for a car, $5,000–7,000. Johnny had great price for Dido, opening from $2,000, $3,000, and $6,000 and closing at $20,000. After all that up and down, we found the car that Dido could use until he had the money to buy a newer car. We found a 2006 Pontiac Torrent and took the car for a rapid test-drive for about five minutes. The car had a problem. All inside car lights were shaking, and all the chairs too. When driving there was no problem. When stopping, the car started to shake. We found that the car had a problem. The dealer told us that they could fix that problem today. Dido and I gave them all day because we went there at 9:00 a.m. We then came back at 3:30 p.m. to check on the problem. When the car was finished, I went to look for insurance. Dido was working from 10:00 a.m. to 5:00 p.m. I went to a new insurance company that opened a couple of days ago. I was searching for a better quote for liability insurance. The agent gave me a quote for the 2006 Pontiac Torrent: $140–230. Then I went to another insurance company, Enterprise Services. I found the same lady who quoted me when I got insurance there. Her name was Cynthia. Cynthia told me that for that Pontiac it would be $180–340. When I was finished with my search for a better insurance quote, I then called Dido to let him know about the options of liability car insurance. Dido made up his mind on which insurance he wanted. I picked him up at his work to do his car paperwork. He paid the $3,000 for a down payment. Johnny told him that he would be paying $300 each month. That was a good deal for Dido. When he started driving his Pontiac, he told me that he liked the car. It is smooth on the road and has had little problems.

Take what you can finish, not what you cannot finish. If you don't finish it, it will finish you. Confidence in yourself will keep you standing taller than the mountains around you. You must believe in yourself. When you want to buy something, do good research on that item or service from different places. Research not once, but twice or more. Walk-in research is better. You get to communicate with a person who has been selling that item or service for a long time. That gives you a heads-up.

I was in a school classroom. A student said to another student, "You will not pass if you don't change how your believe." The attitude that you have must reflect what you want to become and what you want to accomplish. Where do you want to see yourself in one or two years from now? Your dreams should be to climb the mountains of business. Luka Mendez is a friend who used to say negative words about another friend of mine, Sara Chanta. We attended the same high school. For me, it was hard to graduate. After four high schools, I finally graduated at St. Michael Learning Academy. They were both good friends and always treated me great. Surrounding yourself with negative people keeps you negative. Remember that you can change if you are negative. If you are surrounded by negative people, then you need to take evasive action.

This conversation took place at a high school in Houston.

Early in the Morning

Sara: Good morning, Zeit.

Zeit: Good morning, Sara. How are you doing?

Sara: I am doing fine.

Teacher: Good morning, students.

Students: Good morning.

Luka: This place is cold. The ice machine is noisy, bro. Teacher, can I go to the restroom?

Teacher: Let me finish explaining this chapter.

(For the first fifteen minutes, we stay in class. No restroom break.)

Luka: Bro, did you see the fight yesterday?

Zeit: No, I didn't see the fight.

Luka: You always miss the fun, bro. It was on the corner of Hillcraft and Southwest. It was fun. Teacher, can I go now?

Teacher: Yes.

Sara: Zeit, do you understand question four?

Zeit: Yes.

Sara: Can you please help me with it?

Zeit: Sure.

Sara: Zeit! Why does Luka always go to the restroom every morning?

Zeit: I don't know. Maybe we can ask him!

Sara: No, no, no.

Teacher: Luka, can you sit down, please?

Luka: Okay, okay! Bro, this teacher talks crap. We don't need all this reading and writing.

Zeit: Bro, why do you go to the restroom every morning?

Luka: These teachers are explaining nothing. They stand there and talk about crap. We don't have to be here. All this is shit.

Zeit: Really, bro?

Luka: Yup.

Zeit: Bro, you can get yourself a job so that you don't have to waste time here. Or you can get a GED.

At Lunch

Zeit: Bro, let's go to the line.

Luka: I have some cash. I will not eat that food.

Zeit: Let's go to the library.

Luka: No, let's go see those chicks there.

Zeit: Okay, bro.

Luka: Bro, why does Sara always study like a crazy girl?

Zeit: I don't know. Let's go ask her. She is there.

Luka: She is fine, though!

Zeit: Yup.

Zeit: Sara, why do you study a lot?

Sara: I study so that I can go to a good university and have a good job. I need to open a business after my business degree. Luka, what do you want to become?

Luka: What?

Sara: I said, what do you want to become after high school?

Luka: I will do construction.

Sara: Okay.

Sara Chanta is a great, strong woman. She knew what she could fit in and what she couldn't fit in. If she wants something, she looks straight at it and goes for it, with no hesitation. Sara always stays on track. When we are at lunch, you will see her in the library or with her one or two friends. Most of the time, you will see her with a book. She loves reading books and always stays positive. She always tells me that she wants to become a businesswoman. She worked hard in high school, and she has two years left in university. I am proud of her. She is so sweet, accomplishing her goals. That is lovely.

On the other hand, Luka Mendez always keeps himself surrounded with negative words. Apart from me being his friend, he has other friends who follow him around most of the time: Diego, Ado, and Elia, to name the few. They walk in a big group. Luka didn't accomplish his goal to work in a construction company. He didn't follow what he was taught at school. Most of the time, he copied answers from other students. I know right now, wherever he is, he now sees the importance of reading and writing. The key is education. He did not see that in this country, high school education is free. Most of his friends ended up with the same level of standards. Negativity is a disease. Luka now harvests his negative living standard. Sara now harvests her positive standard.

SUCCESS IN THE FOOD TRUCK BUSINESS

Some people have been successful in the food truck business and many other forms of business. Most people end up giving up in this business. Most of the time, they don't understand that success does not come overnight. Research and having connections is very import in business. Having connections is a key to information about the business you are about to start. Information has to be available. Information in business is like trade. When you have a connection with one of the board members of one company, he or she can get you private information but will need something in return: information from your company or advice on how to do something. Having that trade keeps the connection strong. If you don't give that person something in return, there is a 70 percent chance that person will not give you that information again. You have to be humble to some of your connections. Some are running without looking down. You know what happens when you run that way. The fact is that you will fall down somehow, because you were not looking down to see the bumps in the road you are taking.

Some of your connections will want to take advantage of you. Don't let that happen. Be yourself, and let them be them. If you see they are entering deep into your company, then you have to let them know that their noses are smelling more than they are supposed to smell. Be gentle with your connections, even if you want them to lie low. Don't let them see that. So that you can still keep connection. In the food truck business, that is how it goes. All the food trucks have some connections. They sell different foods and drinks, but they still have connections. That helps them know that they need to change their location. They test each other's food, which helps them know how delicious their competitors are.

For our food truck, the Pieanha House, we used to have a good spot where the customers could lie low and enjoy their meals and drinks. We told them stories to keep them around, adding, "See you tomorrow." Some get addicted, and we saw them coming back to buy food again. We had a system where we kept a list of our customers who wanted discounts. The Pieanha House food truck wrote the days of discounts almost to a penny. Those discounts were loved. People liked to eat. Even if they were not hungry, they still wanted to buy food. If you are in the restaurant business, then that should open your eyes. Even if you are planning to open a company of services or selling products, you can apply the same principle. You will be astonished by the good results you will get.

One food truck businessman, named Antonio, had a good food truck. It was lovely and cultivating just by the look of it. He had some good recipes. Antonio used to cook Mexican food. He was selling that food in a location where there were not a lot of Mexicans living there. On the other side was another food truck that sold Italian food. The area was fully populated by Italians. The owner was not Italian, and he didn't speak the language. He simply knew that Italians mostly wanted to eat their food, rather than try new things. The good thing about business is that you don't have to know the language. You simply have to meet the demand, and quality matters. Though language can play a big part, people can still manage. Demand has to meet the need. Antonio didn't succeed in that area because of the food he was selling. Some Italian do eat Mexican food, but the majority always matters in business. You have to sell to the majorities.

Here is one success story of a food truck: Jae Kim. I was already working in the food truck before he went to *Shark Tank*. He started in 2010 and worked hard until having something to present to the sharks. He started a coffee business and then moved to Austin to open a food truck business, selling Korean and Mexican food. Jae became little successful. He attempted twice before he was accepted on *Shark Tank*. He sold Korean barbecue. Jae Kim negotiated 15 percent of his business in exchange for a $600,000 investment in his food truck. He had two choices from the sharks. Barbara Corcoran proposed $600,000 for 30 percent of his business. If you look closer, you see the 15 percent tabled. Jae refused and accepted a offer for 20 percent of his business. Sometimes you have to risk even 5 percent. That has to be calculated.

Jae Kim in His Own Words

This was my third attempt at trying out for *Shark Tank*. It meant so much more because I kept trying, just to have the opportunity to share my vision and passion with the sharks and millions of people around the world.

Keep up connection with the 1 percent. They control 90 percent of the business sphere. They are the rich. If you want to be rich, keep up with the rich. Did you know you can become rich just like Bill Gates, Amancio Ortega, Warren Buffett, Jeff Bezos, Mark Zuckerberg, Larry Ellison, Ingvar Kamprad, Charles Koch, David Koch, and Carlos Slim? Or how about Liliane Bettencourt, Jacqueline Mars, Alice Walton, Maria Franca Fissolo, Susanne Klatten, and don't forget Christy Walton? If you ask any of these rich people, "Is it possible for me to be rich and even pass you?" they will tell you yes. You have to put in more work. Most of these people don't sleep like you. You spend all that valuable time asleep. They work hard twenty-four seven. They don't sleep. Money is not on the tree. Work harder and harder. Don't stop working. Keep yourself healthy.

The key to becoming like them is to start a business, save to invest, and get a mentor who is rich. If you get a poor mentor, where are you going? You are on the track of being poor, not rich. Think rich, just like President Donald Trump and the other rich people. Think a little bit about the words *rich* and *poor*. They definitely sound different. *Rich* has a smooth move with a smile on your face. *Poor* starts with you closing the mouth to the midpoint of your lips, with a scary and awkward face. If your family was poor, don't accept that. Change. Be the lion, not a hyena. Remember to follow the rich believers. You will feel rich even if you have not yet got there. When rich people want to buy something, they first think about it. "Will it benefit me? If it doesn't benefit me, can I sell it?" Those are just a few ways to think. Go out there and get mentors. Don't be scared to ask them about their businesses so that you can see where they are heading. Get mentors who have similarities with what you want to achieve in the future.

THINKING RICH AND ACTING RICH IS THE WAY TO ABUNDANCE

This world is filled with wealthy people. There are about 15.5 millionaires and about 1,900 billionaires in the world. That number is still increasing. All these wealthy people don't sleep. Why? Because money and time don't wait for people. They don't waste time on unimportant matters that will not add something in their knowledge or their wealth. When your attention is on one goal, you must open your ears for some other goals. It doesn't mean that you have to act on it, but stay alert when the market is changing. Wealthy people have this in common. They like brighter futures for themselves, and they don't like to waste time. They always keep their eyes on the prize, and they struggle harder than the poorest people in the world.

Think Like a Rich Person

When you think about your future, what is the first thing comes to mind? Owning a property, or becoming richer than the richest person in the world, Bill Gates? The future is a long-term goal. A lot of strength and sacrifice of your brain and time has to be committed to the short-term goals in order to reach that big goal, your trophy for success. If you meet Bill Gates today and ask him how he became rich, he will tell you that his vision for computers and software didn't rapidly flourish. The vision didn't become a success overnight. And let me tell you this: there is no business that becomes a success in just one night, or even in a month. Years have to be planned. Time has to be invested to the core foundation of the roots of its operation. Bill Gates and other rich people work even harder than a person working in construction. Why do they work harder? Because they understand the word *freedom*. It's the freedom of buying anything they desire in the world, the freedom to live beyond prosperity, and the freedom to not work for other people's dreams. I know you will feel good if you get to drive the car that you want, buy a house or mansion that you will feel good sleeping inside, or get anything that you feel you should have to make your life better. What are you waiting for? Fire up like there is no tomorrow. That urge of success is rooted deeply within you, and it has to be sated in action a little bit.

Time is the single most important commodity in this universe. Wasting time is like counting down from ten to zero. When counting, you finally realize that when you start from ten, you are going down. With any number counted, you lose a value of one of those ten numbers. The same applies to our twenty-four hours. Time is hard to preserve, but those who get to follow the way use the time to do resourceful things. Keeping a list of things to do is a better way to follow up with what you are using your time for. When you have that list in front of your eyes, you no longer have to think about what you are going to do. You have everything written down from morning to evening. List the important things.

Wealthy people always keep up with their time. They keep a folder with papers on what they did each day. When looking at what you did for a week, you can look back to see what you did last week. What was important? What did you accomplish? What was not accomplished? What can you do better? Tracking time is the best thing you can do to achieve most of your goals. That list gives you specific things to do. Don't start thinking about what is next.

Relationships with other people usually get in the way of your time. Friends will show up with problems, family will call about something that just happened, and work will call you. With that list, you have to follow it, not just write it for nothing. If you aren't writing it and following, then it is best not to write it in the first place. It is like a schedule of your old education achievement. When going from elementary to high school and university, or any other degree you have achieve, you follow a time table.

When does this class start, and when does it end? The same thing applies in the real world. When there's a situation where that situation interferes with you list, try to think like a wealthy person. "What is in it for me? Is it worth my time? Do I really have to do this?" Try to be first. Concentrate on going from one objective to another. Go step by step, just like a chameleon.

We all have the best we can do. For some the best they can do is eat what others have worked hard for. Well, that is not you. If it is you, then you should think again. Eating another person's sweat is not uplifting at all. Let's put it to test. When someone buys something or gives you something, do you take good care of it? The answer is that you will not care about the thing so much. You didn't buy it from your money, and so it has no value to you. It is not your sweat. Begin working for what you can call yours. When tomorrow comes, you can say, "This is my property. This is my business. This is my company."

Opportunities are all around us. Most people do not see them. Only a few people grasp the gravity of opportunity. That group of people gets to use those opportunities to their advantage. They keep their eyes open all the time. That is another reason why wealthy people sleep fewer hours. After working hard for those few years, they can relax at the beach. They deserve it. They get to become your boss. They worked harder than a typical person. That is way their achievements are so great. They get even bigger than expected by being the visionary of the idea. Look at Microsoft, Apple, Wal-Mart, Uber, and Starbucks. These huge companies opened other branches of businesses within their companies to help them generate prosperity. When it comes to entertainment, the wealthy people are the ones with money, but they always get to save more than a low class. This creates a divided in by education level, savings, and investment.

Keep Reading

People read for different reasons, but they have common roots. People read to get knowledge. Do you read books frequently? If you do, then keep up the good work of knowledge investment. If you don't like to read, then you'd better get ready to start reading more and more. And thanks for reading this book. Investing in reading is one of the keys to gaining knowledge in your interests. Anthony Trollope once said, "The habit of reading is the only enjoyment I know in which there is no alloy. It lasts when all other pleasures fade. It will be there to support you when all other resources are gone. It will be present to you when the energies of your body have fallen away from you. It will last you until your death It will make your hours pleasant to you as long as you live." There is no better entertainment than reading a book. It doesn't matter how quickly you can read one book. What matters most is the seeds that are planted and the rewards they will bring.

Have a Good Saving Habit

How much have you ever saved? That is a great question to ask. The only class that knows the reason to save is the rich class. They understand the word *harvest*. They understand that in order to get something, they have to give up something. They spend less to save that little bit for the year to come. The poor class only thinks of getting that little and using all of it without saving a penny, and years come and go.

Let's move to health. Rich people get to keep a list things to buy at a grocery store. Poor people tend buy whatever attracts their eyes. Rich people don't go into a grocery store with a list because they can't remember what to buy. They do that to keep track of what they eat and how much. Most of the time, they don't buy things at a corner store. Poor people have less income in a month, yet they are the ones packed in a corner store and mass grocery stores, going in to buy unhealthy foods. The ingredients label shows how the food you buy is unhealthy, yet you still put it in the cart. Taking time to read is inconvenient. You have to keep up with what you buy. Save money for you future resolutions. Try to invest your money in something. Keep change. The money you are saving will make you a billionaire in time. Save us much as you can. Don't worry about the struggle that entangles you every day. Keep up with the good work you're doing by saving. If you don't have a savings account, now is the time. Go get a savings account. You can open as many as you want. All must have a different purpose. Try to prioritize you money. Where do you spend it, and when you should spend it?

NEXT BILLIONAIRE:
THE SUCCESS AHEAD

The world is filled with millionaires. All those millionaires share two things: ambition and desire for more. By having those two things, anyone can stay active, accomplishing milestones and connecting with millionaires. You need to have those connections with millionaires.

Let's make it simple. When you want to go up, you have to start from the bottom. Start with friends of yours who have the same ambitions. Make sure those friends are not letting you down. Stay at the top all the time. If one of those friends lets you down, erase that friend from your important occasions like meeting for success or group talks about your next step in achieving your dreams. When you have those great friends around you, start looking for millionaires who have the same visions and ambitions that you have. Get a rich mentor, not a poor one—unless you want to be poor. Even if you have a couple of thousand dollars, you are still low. There are people who have more than what you have. Don't try to be like them. Have your uniqueness.

When having rich mentors advising on success, keep an open mind. Don't let them take advantage of you, but remember that will have to happen when going to the top. If it was easy to get to the top, then the rich and the poor would be equivalent. No one likes to be poor or stay down. Therefore everyone is trying to get to the top. Men and women are in the same group when it comes to money: the billionaires club, the millionaires club, and the low club. When starting, you have to pass though all those clubs, step by step. If you skip the low club to reach the billionaires club, then you have worked hard with a killing idea, like Mark Zuckerberg. This social media magnate jumped the steps like they didn't exist.

You can have the same type of idea that kills, a brilliant idea that paves the way straight up. Even though that road will not really be straight, you will succumb to those obstacles if you have the ambition to keep working on that idea. Let's put it this way. When you don't have water to drink or are sick, what do you do? You automatically stop what you are doing and attend to the needs of that situation. That is how you should hold you idea close so that it can't be detached from you.

See the Unseen

Keep your eyes open. Don't close them. See the unseen. Don't act on negative thoughts. If you do, then the chance for you to keep old connections will be hard. Going with negative thoughts in leadership or starting your business is heartbreaking in the future. You will lose most of what you have built. The next generation of billionaires is willing to take an idea that will solve something for the majority of people. Technology is booming, and so are the banks. The generation to come will be about advanced technology, environment-friendly businesses, and agriculture industries. From these three divisions, the next billionaires will emerge.

Energy has played a big part of your life. Without energy, there is less chance for that technology to develop. Our bodies use energy, and so do the machines that we make in order to create less manual labor. Everything uses energy. Without energy, there is nothing to exist in this universe. Machines use energy such as geothermal, biomass, solar power, tidal power, and wind power. Countries like Albania, Paraguay, Iceland, Costa Rica, and Norway are already starting to use this form of future environment-friendly energies. These countries use 75–95 percent of their electricity from these great sources of energy. Reduction of pollution is skyrocketing in these countries that are using future energy sources. Gasoline has played a big part in our transportation and electricity, but that era is over. If you ask oil companies about the future of gas, they will let you know that in fifty years, gas will lose value. There is green energy support in many sectors, especially in health, agriculture, and the environment.

Some companies have already started to plan for the future. They are planning how they will change the form of energy that they are using right now. Most are targeted to finish transforming their companies' electrical energies between 2020 and 2030. These companies include Wal-Mart, Apple, Google, Bank of America, Bloomberg LP, Wells Fargo, Coca-Cola Enterprises, BMW Group, Voya Financial, IKEA Group, Autodesk, Facebook, FIA Formula E, Gatwick Airport Limited, General Motors, Goldman Sachs Group, Heathrow Airport, Hewlett Packard Enterprise, HP, Microsoft, ING, Interface, Johnson & Johnson, La Poste, Starbucks, YOOX Group, Pearson, Philips Lighting, Rackspace, Steelcase, Swiss Post, and Tata Motors Limited. Countries are being transformed, and so is your daily life. Governments are saving more money in the energy sector than ever before.

Technology is transforming how we interact in our daily lives, especially in communication, health, and transportation. Companies used to record their important info in books. Now they use spreadsheets and other software. Apps change how we believe. A long time ago, sending a message to your family or friends wasn't easy. You had to send a paper letter. The reply took more than two days. Thanks to the Internet and application developers, we are becoming more social species than ever. You can now call or text in less than two minutes. You can talk to your friends and relatives thanks to Wi-Fi and the Internet. You can exercise at home thanks to the spread of information. You can get news updates more than ever before. The entrepreneur who invests in renewable energy or the advancement of technologies is the one who has opened his or her eyes.

Agriculture is life. No food, no life. Population is increasing at a high rate. There are countries that are starting to create laws for birth control and how many kids one family can have. Some even favor a gender. That is not right. It has been said that we have equal rights. I say genders don't have equal rights. Billionaires of the future are going to emerge from agriculture. Food is needed. Famers that meet the demand of the future population will be the big companies. This lovely dot in this universe has life. Life needs a form of energy to multiply, and that's food plus water. The species on earth need food and water, not Facebook applications. Famers are going to be the banks of the future.

Who Is the Rich Person?

You are the rich person in the world. First you must believe it. It does not matter what is in front of you. You simply have to believe, set the goals, and work hard for those goals. You have ambitions. Go for what you need to go for. You, as the next billionaire, have more work and obstacles to overcome. Rich people are enjoying life after hard work. When you see a rich person, you see good clothes, great smiles, and strength. They have worked. Now they put people to work. You want to be rich? Most rich people will be in these types of businesses: financial services, technology, renewable energy, healthcare, manufacturing, transportation, agriculture and mining, real estate and construction, air transportation, retail and wholesale trade, communications, and renewable energy.

Work hard to achieve those goals and dreams that you have been wanting to achieve. We worked hard in our food truck business. We did what we had to do. We did not fail—we learned a lesson. We learned that failure is the way to learn what to do next. You must not get off your track. Keep going and follow that pathway of success. You can make it if you really want it. Therefore put all your attention and determination on your dreams. Fear is not an option. The sky is the limit.

PHOTO DESCRIPTION

Pieanha House was our food truck. We thought that in this business, we could become independent. Unfortunately, we didn't follow the steps that are needed in business. We don't want you to fail in your business. We have more businesses we are trying. We dedicated this book to the memory of this beautiful food truck, Pieanha House.

Victory: second place with team at a debate competition. We were debating global politics, agriculture, and the future of technology. You can see Tzoc Tetzaguic, Miguel, in the picture.

Note:

As you can see, there were only seven people on the team. That was how this team grew up. We started with only two people. July Romero and John M. Hakizimana started the debate team. Now the team is up to twenty people and continues to grow. If you have a team, keep it up. Don't stop growing. You are the team.

> Agriculture is life. No food, no life. Population is increasing at a high rate.
> —John M. Hakizimana

International debate, Kansas City. Debating politics, economy, and global warming. I always think that I'm too big to fail.

Notes:

My name is Miguel, and I'll share with you my Bible steps.
There are ten important steps that make you a better negotiator. Believe me, we have to used these amazing steps to make a billion dollars. It doesn't have to be millions or billions; it could be thousands, hundreds, or even pennies.

Amadeo Vasquez at a meeting for the next children's basketball competition.

Note:

Amadeo says, "One day I want to have a basketball team of my own. I am working on it and am accomplishing a lot." He wants to be the next Mark Cuban. Despite obstacles, he is getting there.

Printed in the United States
By Bookmasters